Bouncing Back: Turning Redundancy into Opportunity

A Practical Guide to Reinventing Your Career, Building Resilience, and Thriving After Job Loss

PUBLISHED BY: Emmanuel Asiedu

Emmanuel Asiedu

Copyright:© 2024 Emmanuel Asiedu. All rights reserved.

No part of this publication may be reproduced, distributed, or transmitted in any form or by any means, including photocopying, recording, or other electronic or mechanical methods, without the prior written permission of the publisher, except in the case of brief quotations embodied in critical reviews and certain other non-commercial uses permitted by copyright law.

Table of Content

INTRODUCTION 4

My Story: The Early Days 6

Chapter 1: The Reality of Job Security 11

Chapter 2: The Value of Continuous Learning 18

Chapter 3: Navigating the Emotional Challenges of Redundancy 30

Chapter 4: Building a Resilient Career Path 40

Chapter 5: Lessons Learned and Moving Forward 51

Conclusion 61

Thank You for Reading 67

Emmanuel Asiedu

INTRODUCTION

I've had an experience that changed my perspective—a life-altering journey that opened my eyes to new possibilities and made me wiser. It's an experience rooted in reality, one that many people fear: redundancy. Once, I worked as an administrator in a textile printing company in Ghana. I loved what I did, poured my heart into my job, and dreamed of expanding my resume, earning a promotion, and achieving financial stability. But as life often reminds us, things don't always go as planned. Sometimes, the twists and turns we face become the most valuable lessons for our growth and greater achievements.

Robert Kiyosaki, in his book *Rich Dad Poor Dad*, said: *"Life is a teacher. It pushes us around, and each push is a way of telling us to wake up and learn something new."* My push came in the form of redundancy, and it taught me lessons that I carry with me every day—lessons that I believe can benefit you, your family, and your future if you're willing to read on.

I've shared my story countless times with friends, family, and relatives, but in conversations, the brevity often left out the depth of what really happened and the lessons I drew from it. That's why I decided to write this book—not just to tell my story, but to give it the detail it deserves and to use it as a guide for those facing similar challenges. Redundancy isn't a new phenomenon, and yet, it often catches people unprepared. As George Santayana wisely said, *"Those who cannot learn from history are doomed to repeat it."*

This story is my history, and it begins in 2012.

Emmanuel Asiedu

My Story: The Early Days

In June 2012, I was employed as a contract worker after completing six months of probation. I started as a mechanical operator on a Rotary Screen Printing (RSP) machine, where my responsibilities included testing, operating, and troubleshooting machine issues, as well as updating managers on production progress.

I loved my job and worked diligently, often putting in extra hours to meet the financial needs of my family. This routine continued for two years until my health started to decline in May 2014.

I became so ill that I had to take three months off work. During that time, I visited countless doctors and hospitals, but no one could pinpoint the cause of my illness. In desperation, I sought advice from natural healers, herbalists, and medical practitioners, who helped me adopt better eating habits, manage stress, and improve my sleep routines.

Though still unwell, I decided to return to work in July 2014. My boss, upon hearing of my condition, suggested I see the company doctor, Dr. Sarkodie. Initially hesitant, I eventually agreed, and it was one of the best decisions I ever made. Dr. Sarkodie became more than a physician—he became a mentor, guiding me back to health and helping me rebuild my strength. By the end of that year, I was healed and ready to rejoin the workforce.

A New Role, A New Beginning

In October 2014, I transitioned from machine operator to administrator, a position that involved data entry, report writing, and record analysis. I embraced the role and felt like my career was back on track. But in April 2016, the stability I had regained began to crumble.

The Ghanaian economy was slowing, and the textile industry was struggling due to the influx of counterfeit textiles. Major companies were downsizing or shutting down entirely. Our company wasn't immune to the challenges, and by September 2016, the local union had started warning employees of impending layoffs.

By November, the reality of redundancy hit home. One by one, employees were called into meetings and handed termination letters. On November 28, it was my turn. My boss, ever respectful, praised my work but informed me that I was being laid off. Though I wasn't required to leave immediately, the writing was on the wall.

The Emotional Impact of Redundancy

Redundancy was a shock to my system. It wasn't just about losing a job; it felt like losing a part of myself. My mind was consumed with worry about my family, my future, and my ability to bounce back. Mild panic attacks and endless scenarios played out in my head.

I began frantically dropping off resumes at companies, hoping to find a new job. During this time, my family and Dr. Sarkodie provided unwavering support. Their encouragement helped me begin to see redundancy not as a defeat but as a chance to explore new opportunities.

The Turning Point

By December 2016, I realized that redundancy wasn't the end—it was a new beginning. With a few weeks left on payroll, a severance package, and some savings, I decided to take control of my future. I began reflecting deeply on my experiences and the lessons they had taught me.

That's when the idea for this book was born. I wanted to share my story and the wisdom I'd gained, not just for catharsis but to serve as a guide for others facing similar challenges.

Why This Story Matters

Redundancy is a growing reality in a world of economic uncertainty and rapid change. It's a challenge many will face, whether they're students preparing for their first job, employees navigating career shifts, or seasoned professionals caught off guard. My story highlights the importance of preparation, resilience, and adaptability.

Through this experience, I learned to work smarter rather than harder, explore financial options, and seize opportunities rather than relying on luck. I discovered five key lessons that can help anyone prepare for the inevitable challenges of life and career. These lessons aren't just answers—they're guideposts, designed to help you and your loved ones thrive in a world of uncertainty.

Emmanuel Asiedu

Redundancy taught me that setbacks don't define us—they refine us. If you're facing redundancy or anticipating it, know that it's not the end of your journey. It's an opportunity to learn, grow, and build a more resilient future for yourself and your family.

Chapter 1: The Reality of Job Security

In today's rapidly changing job market, one of the most critical lessons I wish I had learned earlier is this: **no job is truly permanent.** This realization can be unsettling, but understanding and preparing for it is essential to building a resilient career. Job security is an idea that many of us take for granted, especially when we're starting out. We're often led to believe that if we work hard, follow the rules, and stay loyal to an organization, our efforts will ensure long-term stability. Unfortunately, this ideal doesn't reflect the realities of modern work environments.

The truth is that companies make decisions based on profitability, market conditions, and shareholder expectations—factors that often have little to do with an individual's performance. Redundancy, restructuring, or downsizing are sometimes inevitable in such situations, leaving even the most dedicated employees vulnerable. Understanding this early can shift your mindset from fear to preparedness, giving you the tools to navigate your career with confidence.

Emmanuel Asiedu

Understanding the Modern Job Market

The concept of lifetime employment, which was once a cornerstone of certain industries, has eroded significantly over the past few decades. Factors such as globalization, rapid technological advancement, and economic fluctuations have created a volatile job market. Roles that were once stable are now disappearing, often replaced by automation or outsourced to regions with lower labor costs.

Take, for example, the banking sector. Not long ago, bank tellers were in high demand. Today, many of those jobs have been replaced by ATMs and online banking systems. Similarly, manufacturing roles have been drastically reduced due to automation and robotics. The rise of artificial intelligence and machine learning means that even jobs in fields like accounting, customer service, and data analysis are increasingly at risk.

For employees, this means adapting to a reality where change is constant and job security is no longer guaranteed. By acknowledging this, you can take proactive steps to safeguard your career.

Redundancy Isn't Personal

One of the most important lessons to internalize is that redundancy is not a reflection of your worth or ability. When I first encountered redundancy, I struggled to separate the decision from my sense of self-worth. It felt personal, as though my contributions and efforts hadn't been valued. This mindset is common but counterproductive.

The truth is that most redundancy decisions are driven by organizational needs, not individual performance. Companies often restructure to cut costs, streamline operations, or adapt to changing markets. For instance, a company that relies heavily on fossil fuels may need to reduce its workforce as it transitions to renewable energy sources. In such cases, even the most talented employees can find themselves affected.

Recognizing that redundancy is a business decision, not a personal slight, helps you maintain perspective. It also allows you to focus on what matters most: planning your next steps and leveraging your experience to create new opportunities.

Emmanuel Asiedu

The Importance of Staying Prepared

Given the uncertainty of job security, preparation is key. One of the most practical steps you can take is to build an emergency fund. This financial cushion acts as a safety net during periods of unemployment, giving you the time and resources to regroup and explore new opportunities without the immediate pressure of financial hardship.

How much should you save?

Financial experts often recommend having three to six months' worth of living expenses saved. This includes rent or mortgage payments, utility bills, groceries, and other essential costs. While this goal may seem daunting, especially early in your career, starting small can make a big difference. Setting aside even a small percentage of your income each month can accumulate over time, providing a valuable buffer in the event of redundancy.

Building a Proactive Career Strategy

Beyond financial preparedness, it's essential to cultivate a proactive approach to your career. This means continuously assessing your skills, staying informed about industry trends, and being open to learning new things. Here are some strategies to consider:

1. **Stay Informed About Your Industry**
   Regularly reading industry news, attending conferences, and engaging with professional networks can help you stay ahead of changes in your field. For example, if you're in marketing, you might explore how artificial intelligence is transforming customer engagement strategies. By understanding these trends, you can position yourself as a forward-thinking professional.

2. **Develop Transferable Skills**
   Transferable skills are abilities that are valuable across various roles and industries. These include communication, problem-solving, leadership, and adaptability. For instance, if you're a project manager in construction, skills like scheduling, budgeting, and team coordination can be applied to other fields like IT or healthcare.

3. **Cultivate a Growth Mindset**
   Embrace the idea that learning is a lifelong process. Whether it's mastering a new software tool, earning a certification, or exploring a

completely new field, being willing to learn can make you more resilient in the face of change.

Case Study: Lessons from Real-Life Redundancy

Let me share an example to illustrate these lessons. A friend of mine, Laura, worked for a mid-sized publishing company for over a decade. She was deeply committed to her role and had built strong relationships with her colleagues. When the company decided to downsize due to declining print revenues, Laura was caught off guard. She hadn't anticipated the possibility of redundancy and found herself scrambling to find a new job.

However, Laura's story didn't end there. She quickly realized the value of her transferable skills—editing, project management, and digital marketing. She invested time in earning a certification in content strategy and began networking through LinkedIn. Within months, she secured a new role at a tech company, where she now oversees their digital content initiatives.

What stood out to me about Laura's journey was her ability to pivot and adapt. By leveraging her existing skills and embracing new opportunities, she turned a challenging situation into a stepping stone for growth.

Redefining Success in a Changing World

Ultimately, understanding the reality of job security is about redefining what success looks like in your career. Success isn't about clinging to a single role or company for decades; it's about staying adaptable, curious, and prepared. It's about viewing change not as a threat but as an opportunity to grow.

While the unpredictability of the modern job market can be intimidating, it also offers the chance to explore new paths, develop diverse skills, and create a more dynamic and fulfilling career. By accepting the reality of job security and taking proactive steps, you can build resilience and thrive in any circumstance.

For those just starting their careers or even seasoned professionals, these lessons serve as a reminder: the best way to navigate uncertainty is with preparation, adaptability, and a mindset focused on growth.

Chapter 2: The Value of Continuous Learning

In a world where industries evolve at lightning speed, one of the most valuable lessons I've learned is the importance of **continuous learning**. Gone are the days when a single degree or qualification could sustain a career for decades. Today, staying relevant in the job market requires an ongoing commitment to upskilling, reskilling, and adapting to new challenges. Continuous learning is not merely a professional obligation—it's an investment in yourself, your career, and your ability to thrive in a competitive and ever-changing world.

This chapter delves into why continuous learning is essential, the benefits it offers, and practical strategies for incorporating it into your life. Whether you're an entry-level employee or a seasoned professional, the principles of lifelong learning can help you remain agile, competitive, and fulfilled in your career.

Why Continuous Learning Matters

Continuous learning is no longer optional—it's a necessity in today's fast-paced, technology-driven job market. The reasons for this shift are rooted in three primary factors:

1. **Technological Advancements**
   With the rise of artificial intelligence, machine learning, and automation, many traditional roles are being transformed or eliminated. For example, data entry jobs are increasingly performed by AI tools, while digital marketing relies heavily on data analytics and automation platforms. Professionals who can adapt to these changes by acquiring relevant technical skills are better positioned to succeed.

2. **Globalization and Competition**
   The interconnectedness of the global economy means that talent pools are no longer limited by geography. Companies can hire skilled workers from anywhere, increasing competition for jobs. To stand out, individuals need to continuously update their skills and demonstrate expertise in emerging areas.

3. **Evolving Career Paths**
   Careers today are no longer linear. Many professionals switch industries, take on freelance

or entrepreneurial roles, or pursue portfolio careers that combine multiple interests. Continuous learning enables individuals to navigate these transitions with confidence.

By embracing the mindset of a lifelong learner, you can future-proof your career, remain relevant in a competitive landscape, and open doors to new opportunities.

The Benefits of Lifelong Learning

Lifelong learning offers a range of benefits that extend beyond professional development. Here are some of the key advantages:

1. **Increased Employability**
   Staying up-to-date with industry trends and acquiring new skills makes you a more attractive candidate to employers. Certifications in emerging fields like data science, digital marketing, or project management can set you apart from competitors.
2. **Adaptability to Change**
   Change is inevitable, but lifelong learners are better equipped to handle it. Whether it's a new

software tool, a shift in company strategy, or a sudden career pivot, a commitment to learning helps you adapt quickly and effectively.

3. **Personal Growth and Confidence**
   Acquiring new knowledge and skills boosts your confidence and expands your perspective. It fosters curiosity and keeps your mind sharp, enhancing both your personal and professional life.

4. **Networking Opportunities**
   Engaging in learning activities, such as attending workshops, conferences, or online courses, often connects you with like-minded professionals. These connections can lead to mentorship opportunities, collaborations, or job referrals.

5. **Career Progression and Salary Growth**
   Professionals who continuously improve their skills are more likely to receive promotions, take on leadership roles, and negotiate higher salaries. Employers value employees who demonstrate a commitment to growth and development.

How to Cultivate a Continuous Learning Mindset

Emmanuel Asiedu

Cultivating a mindset of continuous learning begins with the recognition that education doesn't end after graduation. Here are some practical steps to foster this mindset:

1. **Stay Curious**
   Approach challenges and new experiences with curiosity. Instead of fearing the unknown, see it as an opportunity to learn. Ask questions, seek feedback, and explore topics that intrigue you.

2. **Set Learning Goals**
   Just as you set career goals, create a roadmap for your learning journey. Identify areas where you want to grow, whether it's mastering a specific skill, earning a certification, or exploring a new field.

3. **Embrace Failure as a Learning Opportunity**
   Mistakes are an inevitable part of the learning process. Instead of dwelling on failure, view it as a chance to gain valuable insights and improve.

4. **Prioritize Time for Learning**
   Allocate dedicated time each week for learning activities. Treat it as a non-negotiable part of your schedule, just like work meetings or personal commitments.

Strategies for Lifelong Learning

There are numerous ways to engage in continuous learning, ranging from formal education to informal self-directed activities. Here are some effective strategies:

1. **Enroll in Online Courses and Certifications**
   Online platforms like Coursera, edX, and Udemy offer courses in virtually every field, from coding and digital marketing to leadership and communication. Many of these courses are affordable, flexible, and accessible to learners worldwide.

2. **Attend Workshops and Conferences**
   Industry-specific workshops and conferences provide valuable opportunities to learn from experts, gain hands-on experience, and network with peers. Look for events that align with your professional goals.

3. **Read Widely**
   Books, articles, blogs, and industry reports are excellent resources for staying informed. Dedicate time each week to reading materials that broaden your knowledge and perspective.

4. **Engage in Peer Learning**

   Collaborating with colleagues or joining study groups can enhance your understanding of complex topics. Peer learning encourages discussion, problem-solving, and the exchange of ideas.

5. **Seek Mentorship and Coaching**

   A mentor or coach can provide personalized guidance, share valuable insights, and help you navigate your career. Seek out individuals whose expertise aligns with your learning objectives.

6. **Leverage Technology**

   Use apps, podcasts, and webinars to make learning a seamless part of your daily routine. For example, you can listen to industry podcasts during your commute or watch TED Talks during breaks.

Balancing Learning with a Busy Schedule

One of the biggest challenges of continuous learning is finding time for it amid a busy schedule. Here are some tips to integrate learning into your life without feeling overwhelmed:

1. **Start Small**
   Begin with manageable goals, such as reading one article a day or dedicating 15 minutes to a learning app. Gradually increase your commitment as you build momentum.
2. **Incorporate Learning into Daily Activities**
   Turn idle moments into learning opportunities. For example, listen to audiobooks during your commute or review course materials during lunch breaks.
3. **Focus on Quality Over Quantity**
   It's better to deeply engage with a few meaningful resources than to skim through numerous materials. Choose learning activities that align with your goals and interests.
4. **Leverage Employer-Sponsored Programs**
   Many companies offer training programs, workshops, or tuition reimbursement for employees. Take advantage of these resources to enhance your skills while balancing work responsibilities.
5. **Set Boundaries**
   Protect your learning time by setting boundaries with work and personal commitments.

Communicate your goals to those around you to ensure their support.

Case Study: The Transformative Power of Continuous Learning

Consider the story of Raj, a software engineer who faced redundancy when his company shifted its focus to cloud computing. Recognizing the importance of staying relevant, Raj enrolled in an online course on cloud technologies. He also attended webinars and participated in a local tech meetup group.

Within a year, Raj earned a certification in cloud computing and gained hands-on experience through freelance projects. His proactive approach not only helped him secure a new job but also positioned him as a sought-after expert in his field.

Raj's journey highlights the transformative power of continuous learning. By embracing a growth mindset and leveraging available resources, he turned a challenging situation into an opportunity for advancement.

Overcoming Barriers to Learning

Despite its benefits, continuous learning can feel daunting, especially when faced with obstacles like time constraints, financial limitations, or self-doubt. Here's how to overcome these barriers:

1. **Time Constraints**
    - Break learning activities into smaller, manageable chunks.
    - Use microlearning platforms that deliver bite-sized lessons.
2. **Financial Limitations**
    - Explore free or low-cost resources, such as YouTube tutorials, public library databases, and MOOCs (Massive Open Online Courses).
    - Look for scholarships, grants, or employer sponsorships.
3. **Self-Doubt**
    - Start with beginner-friendly resources to build confidence.
    - Surround yourself with supportive peers who encourage your growth.

Emmanuel Asiedu

The Role of Employers in Promoting Lifelong Learning

Organizations also play a crucial role in fostering a culture of continuous learning. By investing in employee development, companies not only enhance productivity but also boost morale and retention. Here are some ways employers can support learning:

1. **Offering Training Programs**
   Providing access to workshops, seminars, and online courses helps employees stay competitive and engaged.
2. **Encouraging Knowledge Sharing**
   Creating platforms for employees to share insights, such as lunch-and-learn sessions or internal forums, promotes a collaborative learning environment.
3. **Providing Growth Opportunities**
   Offering stretch assignments, cross-training, or job rotations allows employees to develop new skills while contributing to the organization.

Continuous learning is the cornerstone of a successful and fulfilling career. By staying curious, setting goals, and leveraging diverse learning opportunities, you can adapt to change, achieve your aspirations, and unlock your full potential. While the journey requires effort and commitment, the rewards are immeasurable.

In a world where the only constant is change, lifelong learning isn't just a strategy—it's a mindset. Start small, stay consistent, and watch as the knowledge you gain transforms your career and life.

Emmanuel Asiedu

Chapter 3: Navigating the Emotional Challenges of Redundancy

Redundancy is one of the most challenging experiences anyone can face in their professional life. It's not just a loss of income; it's often accompanied by feelings of rejection, fear, and uncertainty about the future. For many, a job is more than a paycheck—it's a source of identity, structure, and purpose. Losing that anchor can be deeply unsettling, especially if the redundancy was unexpected.

However, while redundancy can be emotionally overwhelming, it also presents an opportunity for growth and reinvention. By addressing the emotional challenges head-on, you can navigate this difficult period with resilience and emerge stronger than before. This chapter explores the emotional toll of redundancy, strategies for coping with these feelings, and ways to turn adversity into opportunity.

Understanding the Emotional Impact of Redundancy

Losing a job triggers a range of emotions, often mirroring the stages of grief. Understanding these emotions and recognizing that they're normal can help you process your experience in a healthy way.

1. **Shock and Denial**
   The initial reaction to redundancy is often disbelief. You might find yourself questioning how and why it happened, especially if your performance was strong or the decision seemed abrupt. This stage can be disorienting, as you try to process the sudden change in your circumstances.
2. **Anger and Frustration**
   Anger is a common response to redundancy, particularly if you feel unfairly treated. You might direct this frustration toward your employer, your manager, or even yourself. These feelings can be compounded by the loss of control over your situation.
3. **Fear and Anxiety**
   Concerns about financial stability, career prospects, and the future often set in after the

initial shock. Fear of the unknown can be paralyzing, leading to sleepless nights and heightened stress.

4. **Sadness and Loss**

   Redundancy often brings a sense of loss—not just of the job, but also of the routine, social connections, and sense of purpose it provided. Feelings of sadness or depression may arise as you adjust to this new reality.

5. **Acceptance and Hope**

   Over time, many individuals reach a stage of acceptance, where they begin to see redundancy as an opportunity rather than an ending. This shift in perspective is the first step toward rebuilding and moving forward.

Understanding these emotional stages can help you manage your feelings and recognize that what you're experiencing is a natural response to a significant life event.

Coping with the Emotional Challenges

Managing the emotional toll of redundancy requires both self-compassion and proactive strategies. Here are some steps you can take to navigate this difficult period:

1. **Acknowledge Your Feelings**

   It's essential to give yourself permission to feel whatever emotions arise, whether it's sadness, anger, or fear. Suppressing your feelings can lead to greater stress and hinder your ability to process the experience. Journaling, talking to a trusted friend, or seeking professional counseling can help you explore and validate your emotions.

2. **Avoid Blame and Self-Criticism**

   Many people internalize redundancy as a reflection of their worth or abilities, but it's important to remember that job loss is often a business decision, not a personal failure. Avoid the trap of self-blame and focus on the factors outside of your control.

3. **Seek Support**

   Redundancy can feel isolating, but you don't have to face it alone. Share your feelings with family, friends, or peers who can provide empathy and encouragement. Joining support groups or online communities can also connect you with others who understand your experience.

4. **Create a Routine**

   Losing the structure of a job can be destabilizing. Establishing a daily routine can provide a sense of normalcy and purpose. Set aside time for job searching, skill-building, and self-care activities.

5. **Practice Self-Care**

   Taking care of your physical and mental health is crucial during this time. Prioritize activities that promote well-being, such as exercising, eating nutritious meals, meditating, or spending time in nature. These practices can help reduce stress and improve your resilience.

6. **Reframe Your Perspective**

   While redundancy is undeniably challenging, it can also be a chance to reassess your goals, explore new opportunities, and focus on personal growth. Shifting your mindset from "Why me?" to "What's next?" can help you regain a sense of control.

Embracing the Opportunity for Reinvention

Redundancy often forces individuals to reevaluate their careers and consider paths they may not have explored otherwise. This process of reinvention can be both empowering and transformative. Here's how to embrace it:

1. **Reflect on Your Goals and Values**
   Take time to think about what you truly want from your career. Are there passions or interests you've neglected? Does your previous role align with your values and long-term aspirations? Use this period as an opportunity for self-discovery and realignment.

2. **Identify Transferable Skills**
   Your existing skills and experiences are valuable assets, even if you're considering a career change. Identify skills such as leadership, problem-solving, or project management that can be applied across industries.

3. **Explore New Learning Opportunities**
   Redundancy provides the time and motivation to invest in personal and professional development. Enroll in courses, attend workshops, or pursue certifications that enhance your expertise or prepare you for a new field.

4. **Expand Your Network**
   Reaching out to former colleagues, attending networking events, or connecting with

professionals on LinkedIn can open doors to new opportunities. Building a strong network is key to discovering roles that align with your goals.

5. **Consider Alternative Career Paths**
Redundancy can be a catalyst for exploring alternative work arrangements, such as freelancing, consulting, or starting your own business. These options can offer flexibility and align with your passions and interests.

Lessons from Resilience: Real-Life Stories

Hearing the stories of others who have successfully navigated redundancy can provide inspiration and hope. Consider the story of Emily, a marketing manager who was laid off during a company restructuring. Initially devastated, Emily took time to reflect on her career and realized that she wanted to transition into environmental advocacy—a field she had always been passionate about.

Emily enrolled in a sustainability course, joined local environmental groups, and leveraged her marketing expertise to volunteer for non-profit organizations. Within a year, she secured a role with a prominent environmental NGO, combining her professional skills with her personal values.

Emily's journey illustrates the power of resilience, self-reflection, and proactive planning. By embracing redundancy as an opportunity, she was able to transform a setback into a fulfilling new chapter.

The Role of Emotional Intelligence in Recovery

Emotional intelligence (EI) is a critical skill for navigating the challenges of redundancy. It involves understanding and managing your emotions while also empathizing with others. Here's how to leverage EI during this time:

1. **Self-Awareness**
   Recognize your emotional triggers and responses. Being aware of how redundancy affects you allows you to address those emotions constructively.
2. **Self-Regulation**
   Manage negative emotions by practicing mindfulness and focusing on what you can control. Avoid impulsive reactions and make thoughtful decisions about your next steps.

3. **Empathy**

   Understand that redundancy affects not only you but also your colleagues, family, and friends. Being empathetic can strengthen your relationships and foster mutual support.

4. **Social Skills**

   Use effective communication to maintain connections and build new ones. Networking, collaboration, and active listening are essential for finding opportunities and gaining support.

Moving Forward with Confidence

Recovering from redundancy requires time, effort, and a commitment to self-growth. While the journey may be difficult, it also offers a chance to redefine success and build a more fulfilling career. By addressing the emotional challenges, seeking support, and embracing the opportunity for reinvention, you can emerge from this experience stronger and more resilient.

As you move forward, remember that redundancy doesn't define your worth or potential. It's a chapter in your story,

Bouncing Back

not the conclusion. With the right mindset and actions, you can turn adversity into an opportunity to thrive.

Chapter 4: Building a Resilient Career Path

In an unpredictable world where industries rise and fall, job roles evolve, and economic conditions shift, the concept of career resilience has become more relevant than ever. Career resilience refers to the ability to adapt to challenges, recover from setbacks, and continuously thrive in a dynamic job market. Building a resilient career path is about more than securing the next paycheck—it's about preparing for long-term growth, adaptability, and fulfillment.

This chapter explores the strategies and mindset needed to create a career that can withstand challenges such as redundancy, technological shifts, and changing market demands. It emphasizes the importance of embracing adaptability, cultivating diverse skills, and taking proactive steps to future-proof your professional journey.

Understanding Career Resilience

Career resilience is a blend of mindset, skillset, and strategy. It's the ability to navigate the twists and turns of a professional journey with a sense of purpose and confidence. This resilience is built on several key principles:

1. **Adaptability**
   Resilient professionals are open to change and flexible in their approach. They view challenges as opportunities to learn and grow rather than insurmountable obstacles.
2. **Self-Awareness**
   Understanding your strengths, weaknesses, values, and goals is essential for navigating career decisions. Self-aware individuals are better equipped to make choices that align with their long-term aspirations.
3. **Continuous Learning**
   The commitment to lifelong learning ensures that you remain relevant and competitive in an ever-evolving job market.
4. **Proactive Planning**
   Resilient professionals don't wait for challenges to arise; they anticipate potential disruptions and prepare accordingly.

By embracing these principles, you can cultivate a career path that is not only resilient but also deeply fulfilling.

The Role of Adaptability in Career Resilience

Adaptability is perhaps the most critical trait for building a resilient career. In a rapidly changing job market, the ability to pivot and embrace new opportunities is invaluable. Here's how to develop and leverage adaptability:

1. **Embrace Change**
   Change can be intimidating, but it's also inevitable. Resilient professionals view change as a natural part of their journey and an opportunity for growth. For example, if your industry is shifting toward digitalization, consider how you can acquire relevant skills to stay ahead.
2. **Stay Open to Learning**
   Being adaptable means being willing to learn new tools, techniques, and ways of working. This could involve enrolling in courses, attending workshops, or experimenting with new technologies.

3. **Think Outside the Box**

   Adaptability often requires creative problem-solving. Instead of dwelling on what's lost during a career setback, focus on what's possible. Consider alternative career paths or ways to apply your existing skills in new contexts.

4. **Maintain a Growth Mindset**

   A growth mindset is the belief that abilities can be developed through effort and learning. This mindset fosters resilience by encouraging you to see challenges as opportunities to improve.

Cultivating a Diverse Skill Set

One of the most effective ways to build career resilience is by cultivating a diverse skill set. The broader your range of skills, the more opportunities you'll have to pivot and thrive in a changing job market.

1. **Develop Transferable Skills**

   Transferable skills, such as communication, problem-solving, and leadership, are valuable across industries. These skills make it easier to transition between roles or sectors.

2. **Balance Hard and Soft Skills**

    Hard skills (e.g., coding, data analysis) are crucial for technical proficiency, while soft skills (e.g., emotional intelligence, teamwork) enhance collaboration and adaptability. Strive to develop a balance between the two.

3. **Stay Ahead of Industry Trends**

    Research emerging trends and technologies in your field. For example, if you work in marketing, understanding data analytics or artificial intelligence can set you apart from the competition.

4. **Experiment with Side Projects**

    Pursuing side projects or hobbies can help you develop new skills in a low-pressure environment. For instance, creating a blog or podcast can enhance your communication and digital marketing skills.

Proactive Career Planning

Resilient professionals don't leave their careers to chance—they actively plan and prepare for the future. Proactive career planning involves setting goals, anticipating challenges, and taking strategic steps to achieve long-term success.

1. **Set Clear Goals**
   Define what success looks like for you. Whether it's achieving a leadership position, transitioning to a new industry, or maintaining work-life balance, having clear goals provides direction and motivation.

2. **Regularly Assess Your Career**
   Periodically review your career progress and reassess your goals. Are you on track to achieve what you want? Are there new opportunities or challenges you need to address?

3. **Build a Strong Professional Network**
   Networking isn't just about finding your next job—it's about building relationships that can provide guidance, mentorship, and support. Attend industry events, engage with peers on LinkedIn, and seek out opportunities to collaborate.

4. **Create a Career Backup Plan**
   Consider what you would do if faced with redundancy or a significant career shift. Having a backup plan can provide peace of mind and reduce stress during uncertain times.

Future-Proofing Your Career

Future-proofing your career means preparing for changes before they occur. This proactive approach ensures that you remain competitive and relevant in the job market, no matter what challenges arise.

1. **Stay Informed About Market Trends**
   Read industry news, follow thought leaders, and participate in professional forums. Understanding where your industry is headed allows you to adapt your skills and strategies accordingly.
2. **Invest in Education and Training**
   Regularly update your knowledge through certifications, workshops, or advanced degrees. For instance, if you're in finance, learning about blockchain technology can enhance your expertise.
3. **Diversify Your Career Portfolio**
   Consider developing multiple streams of income or areas of expertise. For example, you could pursue freelance work, consulting, or teaching in addition to your primary role.
4. **Embrace Technology**
   Familiarize yourself with tools and platforms that

are transforming your field. Even basic proficiency in widely used software can enhance your employability.

Building Resilience During Career Setbacks

Career setbacks, such as redundancy, rejection, or missed promotions, are inevitable. However, how you respond to these setbacks can define your long-term success.

1. **Accept and Process the Setback**
   Acknowledge your feelings and give yourself time to process the disappointment. Suppressing emotions can lead to burnout, while acceptance allows you to move forward.
2. **Identify Lessons Learned**
   Every setback is an opportunity to learn and grow. Reflect on what went wrong and how you can improve. For example, if you didn't get a job you applied for, consider seeking feedback to identify areas for development.
3. **Seek Support**
   Reach out to mentors, friends, or career coaches who can provide guidance and encouragement.

Having a support system can make it easier to navigate challenges.

4. **Refocus on Your Goals**
   Use the setback as a chance to reassess your priorities and realign your efforts. Sometimes, setbacks can lead to unexpected opportunities that are better aligned with your long-term aspirations.

Real-Life Stories of Career Resilience

To illustrate the power of career resilience, consider the story of Carlos, a mid-level manager in the retail industry. When his company filed for bankruptcy, Carlos faced redundancy after 15 years in his role. While initially devastated, he decided to view the situation as an opportunity for reinvention.

Carlos enrolled in an online MBA program and began networking with professionals in the tech sector. He identified transferable skills, such as operations management and team leadership, that were valuable in other industries. Within two years, Carlos secured a role in supply chain management at a growing e-commerce company, combining his retail experience with his new qualifications.

Carlos's journey underscores the importance of adaptability, learning, and proactive planning in building career resilience.

The Emotional Side of Career Resilience

Resilience isn't just about skills and strategies—it's also about mindset and emotional strength. Building emotional resilience can help you navigate career challenges with confidence and grace.

1. **Cultivate Self-Belief**
   Believe in your ability to overcome obstacles and achieve your goals. Positive self-talk and visualization can help reinforce this belief.
2. **Practice Gratitude**
   Focus on the positives in your life and career, even during challenging times. Gratitude can improve your mental well-being and provide perspective.
3. **Stay Connected**
   Maintain strong relationships with family, friends,

and colleagues. A supportive network can provide encouragement and advice during tough times.

4. **Seek Professional Help When Needed**
   If career setbacks take a toll on your mental health, don't hesitate to seek professional counseling or therapy. Emotional well-being is a crucial component of career resilience.

Building a resilient career path is an ongoing process that requires adaptability, proactive planning, and a commitment to lifelong learning. By cultivating diverse skills, staying informed about industry trends, and embracing a growth mindset, you can navigate challenges and create a fulfilling professional journey.

Resilience doesn't mean avoiding setbacks—it means bouncing back stronger. With the right mindset and strategies, you can turn obstacles into opportunities and achieve long-term success in a dynamic and unpredictable world.

Chapter 5: Lessons Learned and Moving Forward

The end of a challenging chapter in your career, such as redundancy or a period of uncertainty, can feel overwhelming. However, it also provides an invaluable opportunity for reflection, growth, and a chance to move forward with newfound clarity and purpose. Chapter 5 focuses on the lessons learned from adversity and outlines actionable steps to build a brighter, more fulfilling future.

This chapter will guide you through consolidating what you've learned, setting meaningful goals, embracing reinvention, and paying it forward by helping others navigate similar challenges.

Reflecting on Lessons Learned

Periods of career turbulence often teach us lessons that shape our professional journey in profound ways. Taking time to reflect on what you've learned is an essential step in moving forward. Below are some key lessons that many people discover during challenging times:

1. **Adaptability is Crucial**

   One of the most valuable lessons from any career setback is the importance of adaptability. The ability to pivot and adjust your approach when circumstances change is a skill that will serve you throughout your career.

2. **Redundancy is Not the End**

   Experiencing redundancy or a career setback doesn't define your worth or capabilities. Instead, it can act as a reset, giving you the opportunity to explore paths you may not have considered before.

3. **Networks Matter**

   The relationships you build with colleagues, mentors, and peers often prove invaluable during career transitions. A strong network can provide support, guidance, and access to new opportunities.

4. **Lifelong Learning is Essential**

   Keeping your skills sharp and staying open to new knowledge equips you to navigate changes in your industry or even transition into entirely new fields.

5. **Self-Care is Non-Negotiable**

   Career challenges can take a toll on your mental and physical health. Prioritizing self-care ensures you maintain the energy and resilience needed to move forward.

Reflecting on these lessons will not only help you process your experiences but also empower you to approach the future with confidence.

Setting Meaningful Goals

Once you've reflected on your experiences, the next step is to set clear, achievable goals that align with your values and aspirations. Goal setting provides direction and motivation, helping you stay focused as you navigate the next phase of your career.

1. Define Your Priorities

Ask yourself what truly matters to you. Are you seeking financial stability, creative fulfillment, work-life balance, or opportunities to make a meaningful impact? Understanding your priorities will guide your goal-setting process.

2. Set SMART Goals

SMART goals are specific, measurable, achievable, relevant, and time-bound. For example, instead of saying, "I want to learn new skills," a SMART goal would be, "I will complete an online course in project management within three months."

3. Break Goals into Actionable Steps

Large goals can feel overwhelming, so break them into smaller, manageable tasks. For instance, if your goal is to transition to a new industry, your steps might include researching roles, networking with professionals, and updating your resume.

4. Regularly Review and Adjust Your Goals

Life is dynamic, and your goals may need to evolve as circumstances change. Regularly reviewing your progress and adjusting your objectives ensures they remain relevant and achievable.

5. Celebrate Milestones

Acknowledging and celebrating small wins along the way boosts motivation and reinforces your commitment to your larger goals.

Embracing Reinvention

Career setbacks often act as catalysts for reinvention. This is a chance to redefine your professional identity, explore new interests, and pursue opportunities that align with your values and passions.

Exploring New Directions

Consider what aspects of your previous roles you enjoyed and what left you feeling unfulfilled. This reflection can help you identify new directions to explore. For instance, if you loved mentoring colleagues, you might consider a role in training or education.

Acquiring New Skills

Reinvention often involves developing new skills to match your career aspirations. Enroll in courses, attend workshops, or seek certifications that align with your goals. For example, transitioning into tech might require learning programming languages or gaining proficiency in tools like Tableau or Python.

Experimenting with Side Projects

Side projects or freelance work can allow you to test new career paths without making an immediate commitment. For instance, starting a blog, offering consulting services, or volunteering in your community can provide valuable experience and insights.

Embracing Entrepreneurial Opportunities

For some, reinvention may involve starting a business. This path requires courage, planning, and perseverance, but it can also offer unparalleled creative freedom and fulfillment.

Building a Resilient Career Mindset

Reinvention and growth require not only skills but also the right mindset. Developing a resilient career mindset involves cultivating attitudes and habits that help you thrive amid uncertainty.

Adopt a Growth Mindset

A growth mindset is the belief that skills and abilities can be developed through effort and learning. Embracing this perspective allows you to view challenges as opportunities for improvement.

Practice Gratitude

Focusing on what you have, rather than what you lack, can shift your perspective and foster a sense of abundance. Gratitude can improve your emotional resilience and keep you motivated.

Stay Curious

Curiosity drives exploration and innovation. Staying curious about trends, industries, and new ways of working can lead to unexpected opportunities.

Develop Emotional Intelligence

Emotional intelligence (EI) is the ability to understand and manage your own emotions while empathizing with others. Strong EI helps you build relationships, handle stress, and navigate complex workplace dynamics.

Paying It Forward

Once you've learned valuable lessons and rebuilt your career, consider paying it forward by helping others who are navigating similar challenges. Sharing your experiences and offering support can create a positive ripple effect, both personally and professionally.

Mentoring

Becoming a mentor allows you to guide others through their career journeys. Share your insights, provide constructive feedback, and help them navigate challenges with confidence.

Volunteering Your Expertise

Offer your skills and knowledge to non-profits, community organizations, or educational institutions. This not only benefits others but also enhances your own sense of purpose and fulfillment.

Sharing Your Story

Writing articles, giving talks, or participating in panels about your career journey can inspire and educate others. By sharing how you overcame challenges, you can provide hope and practical advice.

Supporting Peer Networks

Actively engage in professional communities or networks, contributing ideas, resources, and encouragement. Building a culture of mutual support strengthens the entire network.

Case Study: Turning Lessons Into Triumph

Consider the story of Priya, a mid-career professional in the publishing industry who faced redundancy when her company shifted to digital platforms. Initially devastated, Priya used the experience as an opportunity to reflect on her career. She realized she had always been passionate about storytelling, regardless of the medium.

Priya enrolled in a course on digital content creation and began freelancing as a content strategist. She also started mentoring young professionals interested in writing and publishing. Over time, Priya built a thriving business helping brands craft compelling narratives. Today, she views her redundancy not as a setback but as the beginning of an exciting new chapter.

Emmanuel Asiedu

Priya's story illustrates how reflecting on lessons, setting meaningful goals, embracing reinvention, and giving back can transform a challenging experience into a source of growth and success.

Moving forward after a career challenge is about more than just finding your next job—it's about learning from the experience, setting a course for the future, and growing into the best version of yourself. By reflecting on the lessons learned, setting meaningful goals, embracing reinvention, and cultivating resilience, you can navigate any obstacle with confidence and purpose.

Remember, your career is a journey, not a destination. Each setback and success is an opportunity to learn, grow, and create a fulfilling professional life. And as you move forward, don't forget the power of paying it forward—sharing your knowledge and experiences can inspire and empower others to navigate their own journeys.

Conclusion

From Redundancy to Reinvention—A Journey of Growth and Impact

Redundancy is often seen as a devastating blow, a moment that turns your world upside down. I know this because I've been there. I've felt the uncertainty, the fear, and the weight of the unknown. Yet, looking back now, I realize that redundancy wasn't the end—it was the beginning of a new chapter, one that allowed me to rediscover myself, reinvent my career, and make a meaningful impact on others facing similar challenges.

After being made redundant from my role in the textile industry, I found myself at a crossroads. At first, the loss felt overwhelming, but it also gave me a moment to pause and reflect on my life and career. I realized that this wasn't just an opportunity to find another job—it was a chance to redefine success and align my future with my passions and values.

This realization led me to venture into entrepreneurship. Drawing from my own experiences, I decided to dedicate myself to helping others navigate the difficult terrain of job loss. I began offering guidance, sharing lessons I'd learned, and creating resources like this ebook to empower individuals to bounce back after redundancy.

Venturing into Entrepreneurship and Making an Impact

Becoming an entrepreneur wasn't just a career decision—it was a calling. I wanted to turn my personal challenges into a platform for change, a way to give back to those who, like me, were grappling with the uncertainties of job loss.

Through my initiatives, I've had the privilege of supporting countless individuals as they rebuild their careers, find new opportunities, and regain their confidence. Whether through workshops, one-on-one coaching, or online content, my goal has always been to provide practical tools and encouragement to those who need it most.

The impact has been profound. I've seen people transition from despair to hope, from uncertainty to clarity, and from redundancy to success. Hearing their stories and witnessing their growth has been one of the most rewarding aspects of my journey.

Lessons Learned on the Path to Reinvention

Through my own experiences and the work I've done with others, I've come to understand some universal truths about bouncing back from redundancy:

1. **Redundancy is a Reset, Not an End:** Job loss is challenging, but it's also a chance to reimagine your career and explore new possibilities.
2. **Your Value is Greater Than Any Job Title:** Redundancy doesn't define your worth. Your skills, experience, and potential remain intact.
3. **Invest in Yourself:** Lifelong learning and skill-building are essential for staying relevant and competitive in today's ever-changing job market.
4. **Build Resilience:** Setbacks are inevitable, but resilience helps you navigate them with strength and determination.
5. **Lean on Your Network:** Family, friends, and professional connections can provide guidance, support, and new opportunities.

Emmanuel Asiedu

How You Can Bounce Back and Thrive

If you've experienced redundancy or fear it might happen, know that you're not alone—and you're not powerless. Here's how you can take control of your journey:

- **Reflect on Your Goals:** Use this time to reassess what you truly want from your career and life. Redundancy can be an opportunity to align your actions with your passions and values.
- **Embrace Learning:** Invest in new skills and knowledge that can open doors to new industries or roles. Online courses, workshops, and certifications are excellent resources.
- **Network with Purpose:** Reach out to former colleagues, mentors, and industry professionals. Networking can lead to opportunities you may not have considered.
- **Consider Entrepreneurship:** Like me, you may find that starting your own business or freelancing offers the freedom and fulfillment you've been seeking.

- **Stay Positive and Persistent:** Remember, every challenge is an opportunity to grow. Keep moving forward, even when the path feels uncertain.

Your Story is Still Being Written

Redundancy was a turning point in my life, one that pushed me to grow, adapt, and discover new possibilities. Today, I am proud to use my experiences to help others find their footing, build resilience, and chart their own paths to success.

My journey is proof that redundancy doesn't have to be the end. It can be the beginning of something incredible— a chance to reinvent yourself, pursue your dreams, and make an impact on others.

To anyone facing job loss, I want you to know this: You are not defined by this moment. You have the strength, the skills, and the potential to bounce back and build a future that excites and fulfills you. Take the lessons from this ebook, apply them to your own journey, and remember—your best chapters are still ahead.

Emmanuel Asiedu

Thank you for allowing me to share my story with you. Together, let's turn challenges into opportunities and create a brighter, more resilient future.

Thank You for Reading

I hope you've found immense value in this ebook and that it has given you practical insights into navigating redundancy and building a resilient career. Most importantly, I hope the lessons shared have resonated with you and inspired a fresh perspective on overcoming challenges in the workplace.

Thank you for taking time out of your busy schedule to read this material—it means a lot to me. If these ideas make sense to you and you've enjoyed what you've read, I'd love to hear your thoughts! Please consider:

- Reaching out to me directly via email at **emmanuelasiedu84@gmail.com**. I personally read every comment and email, so feel free to drop me a message, even if it's just to say hello!

If you'd like to connect further, you can also follow me on **Twitter, LinkedIn, Instagram**, and join the conversations on my **Facebook Fan Page**. Let's continue building a community where we share ideas and uplift one another.

Lastly, I want to take a moment to emphasize the effort and dedication that went into creating this ebook. If you believe it could help someone you know, please encourage them to purchase it through my sales page rather than distributing it for free. This ensures I can continue providing valuable resources to readers like you.

Once again, thank you for your time and support. I wish you nothing but success as you move forward in your career and life. Remember, redundancy is not the end—it's a new beginning filled with opportunities.

Warm regards,
Emmanuel Asiedu

www.ingramcontent.com/pod-product-compliance
Lightning Source LLC
Chambersburg PA
CBHW070410230526
45471CB00006B/2739